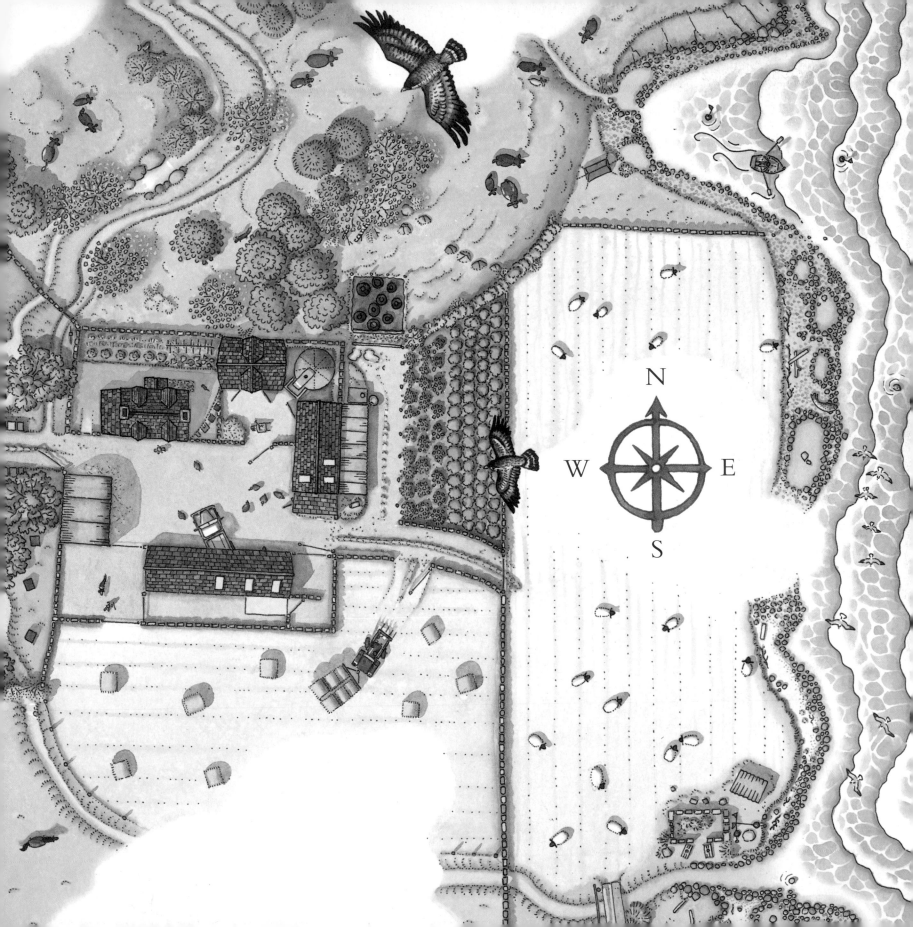

For Rose and Mike

OXFORD
UNIVERSITY PRESS

Great Clarendon Street, Oxford OX2 6DP

Oxford University Press is a department of the University of Oxford.
It furthers the University's objective of excellence in research, scholarship,
and education by publishing worldwide in

Oxford New York

Athens Auckland Bangkok Bogotá Buenos Aires
Cape Town Chennai Dar es Salaam Delhi Florence Hong Kong Istanbul
Karachi Kolkata Kuala Lumpur Madrid Melbourne Mexico City Mumbai
Nairobi Paris São Paulo Shanghai Singapore Taipei Tokyo Toronto Warsaw

with associated companies in Berlin Ibadan

Oxford is a registered trade mark of Oxford University Press
in the UK and in certain other countries

Copyright © Benedict Blathwayt 2001

The moral rights of the author/artist have been asserted

Database right Oxford University Press (maker)

First published 2001

British Library Cataloguing in Publication Data available

Hardback ISBN 0–19–910672-X
Paperback ISBN 0–19–910673-8

1 3 5 7 9 10 8 6 4 2

Printed in Italy

Benedict Blathwayt

In the
Country

OXFORD

UNIVERSITY PRESS

This is where we live

field

valley

forest

wood

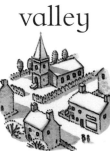

village

beach

stream

waterfall

hill

cliff

road

mountain

This is our farm

barn

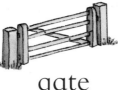

farmhouse

stable

gate

cow shed

pond

silo

sheep-dip

fence

wall

hen house

bridge

9

There is work for us all

bucket

sheepdog

plough

seed drill

wheelbarrow

broom

tractor

baler

hoe

shovel

pick-up truck

shepherd

rake

fork

Spring is here

blossom

bumble-bee

bud

shoots

caterpillar

nest

frog

duckling

rainbow

lamb

frog spawn

tadpoles

dragonfly

ladybird

Animals around the farm

sheep

rabbit

hen

duck

cockerel

cow

pony

swallow

cat

fox

hawk

deer

15

A trip in the boat

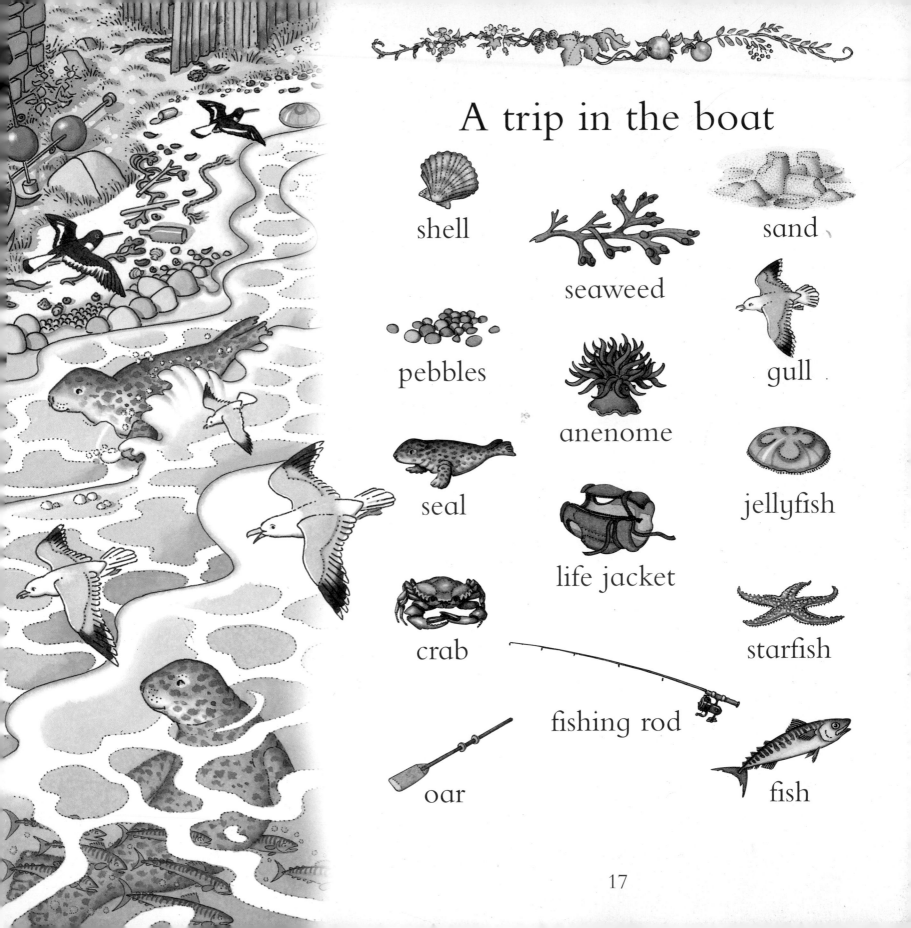

shell

seaweed

sand

pebbles

anenome

gull

seal

life jacket

jellyfish

crab

starfish

fishing rod

oar

fish

17

Hot summer days

lizard

swimming

sailing

butterfly

wheat

grasshopper

straw

poppy

harvest mice

beetle

pheasant

combine harvester

19

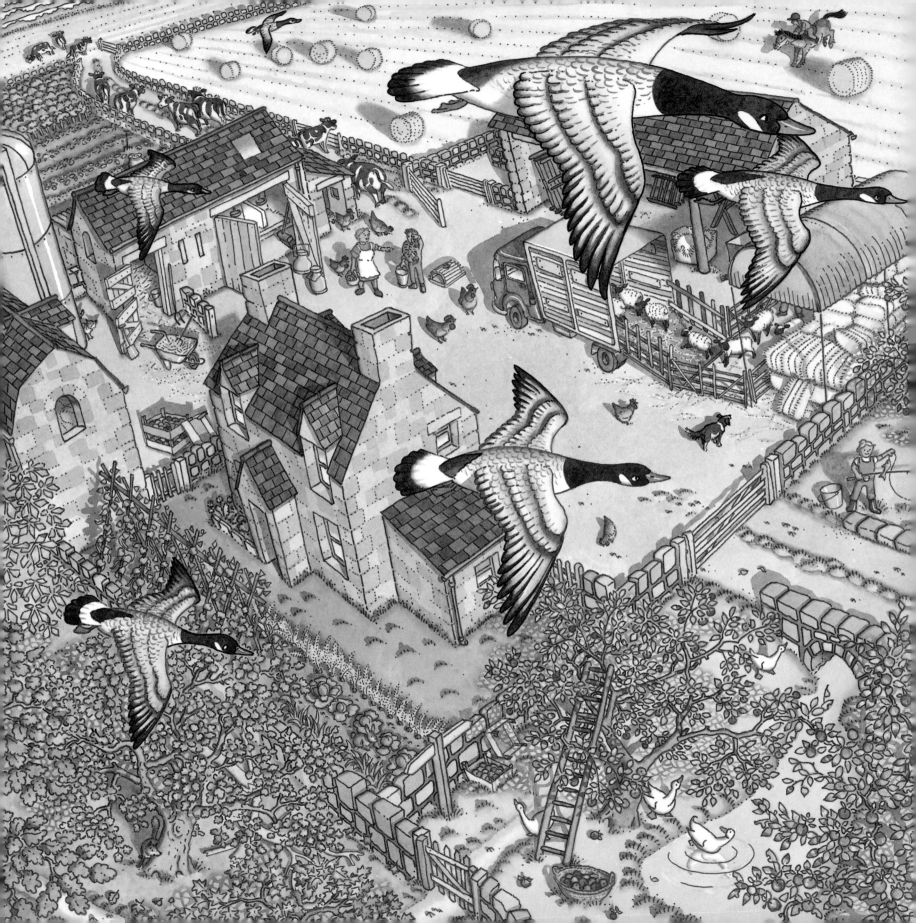

Food from our farm

eggs

potatoes

milk

cheese

honey

pumpkin

apples

maize

cabbage

carrots

beans

apple juice

21

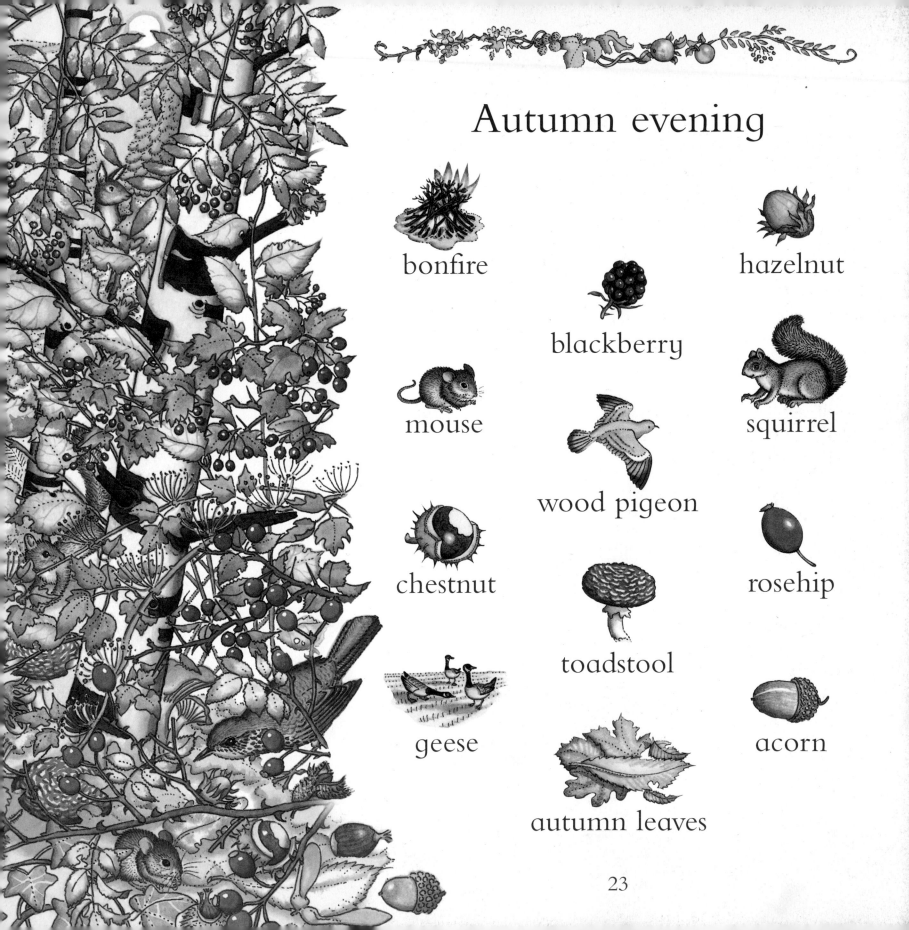

Autumn evening

bonfire

hazelnut

blackberry

mouse

squirrel

wood pigeon

chestnut

rosehip

toadstool

geese

acorn

autumn leaves

When winter winds blow

snow

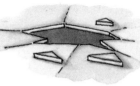

ice

lamp

logs

hay bale

boots

saw

woollen hat

axe

manger

gloves

owl

25

Index

Index

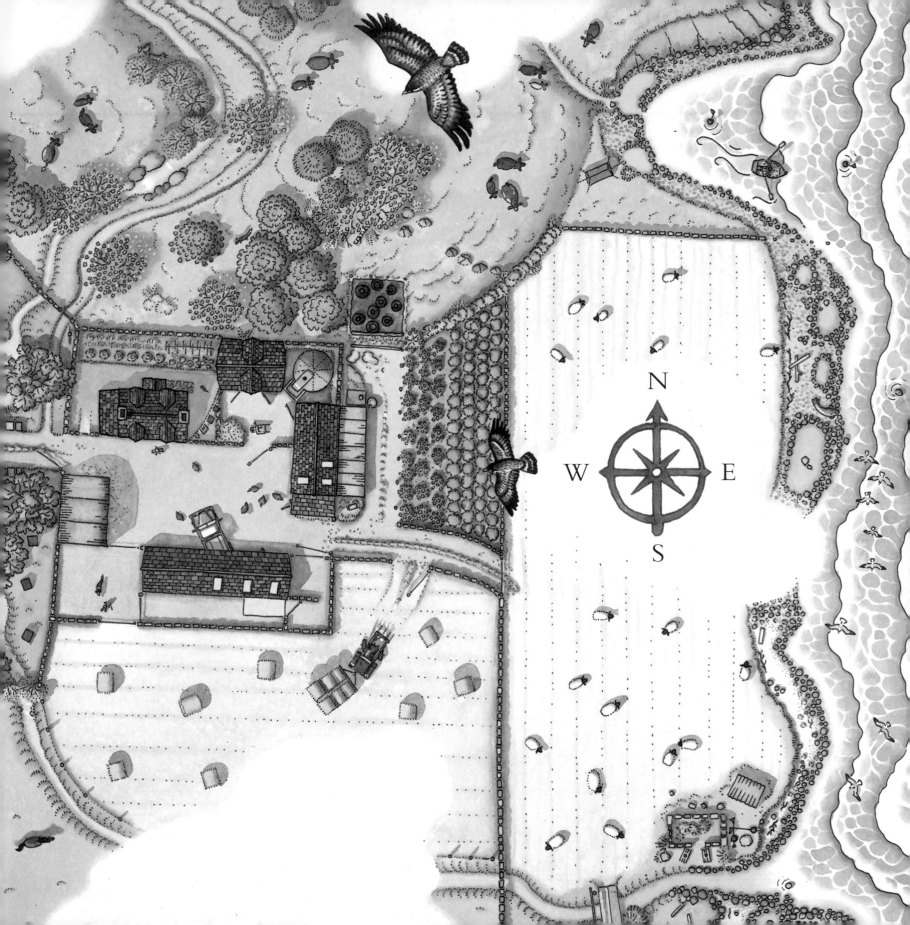